Biographies

LEWIS and CLARK

by Jason Glaser

Consultant:

Harry W. Fritz, PhD
Professor of History
University of Montana
Missoula, Montana

Capstone
press

Mankato, Minnesota

Fact Finders is published by Capstone Press
151 Good Counsel Drive, P.O. Box 669, Mankato, Minnesota 56002
www.capstonepress.com

Library of Congress Cataloging-in-Publication Data
Glaser, Jason.
    Lewis and Clark / by Jason Glaser.
    p. cm.—(Fact finders. Biographies)
    Includes bibliographical references and index.
    ISBN 0-7368-2665-3 (hardcover)
    1. Lewis, Meriwether, 1774–1809—Juvenile literature. 2. Clark, William, 1770–1838—Juvenile
literature. 3. Explorers—West (U.S.)—Biography—Juvenile literature. 4. Lewis and Clark Expedition
(1804–1806)—Juvenile literature. 5. West (U.S.)—Discovery and exploration—Juvenile literature. [1.
Lewis and Clark Expedition (1804–1806) 2. Lewis, Meriwether, 1774–1809. 3. Clark, William,
1770–1838. 4. Explorers. 5. West (U.S.)—Discovery and exploration] I. Title. II. Series.
F592.7.L42G58 2005
973.4′6′092—dc22   2003026874

Summary: An introduction to the lives of explorers Meriwether Lewis and William Clark, who
    played an important role in the history of the United States.

Editorial Credits
Megan Schoeneberger, editor; Juliette Peters, series designer; Patrick D. Dentinger, book
    designer and illustrator; Erin Scott, Sarin Creative, map illustrator; Kelly Garvin, photo
    researcher; Eric Kudalis, product planning editor

Photo Credits
Art Resource, NY/National Portrait Gallery, Smithsonian Institution, 21; The New York Public
    Library, 23
Charles Willson Peale/Independence NHP, 9
Corbis/David Muench, 24–25
Getty Images/Hulton Archive, 8, 12, 16, 18–19
Jefferson National Expansion Memorial/National Park Service, 17
Library of Congress, 10–11
North Wind Picture Archives, cover (both), 1 (both), 4–5, 6–7, 22
Painting "Lewis and Clark: The Departure from the Wood River Encampment, May 14, 1804"
    by Gary R. Lucy. Courtesy of the Gary R. Lucy Gallery Inc.-Washington, MO, 14–15
Yale Collections of Western Americana, Beinecke Rare Book and Manuscript Library, 13

1 2 3 4 5 6 09 08 07 06 05 04

Table of Contents

Chapter 1

Two Rivers

In June 1805, Meriwether Lewis, William Clark, and their crew stood on the riverbank. Two rivers spread out before them. To the north, water crashed over sharp rocks. To the south, the water ran clear. Which was the Missouri River?

The crew needed to follow the Missouri River. The wrong choice meant wasted days, maybe months, of hard work. Time was valuable. They needed to reach the Pacific Ocean before winter.

Lewis and Clark decided to split up for the day. Clark and a few men headed south. The others followed Lewis to the north. Everyone met again that night.

The Great Falls on the Missouri River was a landmark for Lewis and Clark.

Clark's group had heard waterfalls. The Mandan Indians had told the group about the Great Falls on the Missouri River. Lewis and Clark knew to go toward the waterfalls. Their journey to the Pacific Ocean could go on.

Chapter 2

Men of Courage

William Clark was born in Virginia in 1770. Clark's family moved to present-day Kentucky in 1784.

Clark's family and other settlers fought against the American Indians in the Ohio River valley. The settlers wanted to move the Indians out of the area. U.S. soldiers joined the fight. They fought many times over the right to live on the land.

In 1774, Meriwether Lewis was born in Virginia. He became a good friend of his neighbor, Thomas Jefferson. When Lewis was young, he and Jefferson sent messages to each other from a distance by flashing mirrors.

American Indians and U.S. soldiers fought many battles over land in the Ohio River valley.

▲ Meriwether Lewis was a skilled shooter.

FACT!

Lewis designed his own rifle. It was so good that the U.S. Army copied it.

Becoming Soldiers

Lewis grew up during the Revolutionary War (1775–1783). His father fought against the British. Lewis was proud of his father, who died in the war. Lewis wanted to be a soldier like his father. When Lewis was 18 years old, he joined the army.

Clark also enjoyed battle. He liked excitement. Clark joined the U.S. Army when he was 22 years old.

Lewis was good with rifles. In 1795, Lewis moved to a different army unit. There, he met Clark. They became good friends.

Clark was a good leader, but he often felt very sick. Stomach pains made it hard for him to lead soldiers in tough exercises.

After four years, Clark retired from the army. Still, he exchanged letters with Lewis and other friends from the army.

William Clark was an officer in the U.S. Army. ▶

Chapter 3

Looking West

In the late 1700s, people wondered if a great river flowed across North America. People hoped a river joined the Atlantic Ocean to the Pacific Ocean. Traders and settlers could follow such a river across the West. This river would be known as the Northwest Passage.

Thomas Jefferson became president in 1801. Jefferson wanted to find the Northwest Passage. He wanted the United States to control it. Jefferson planned to send explorers to find the source of the Missouri River. From there, they would look for a river that could take them all the way to the Pacific Ocean.

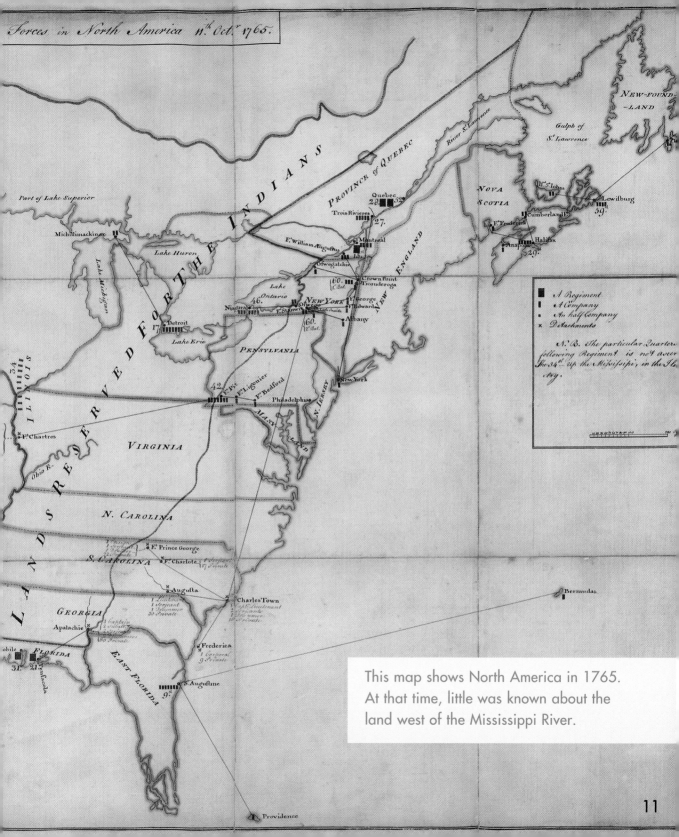

Forces in North America 11th Octr. 1765.

This map shows North America in 1765.
At that time, little was known about the
land west of the Mississippi River.

11

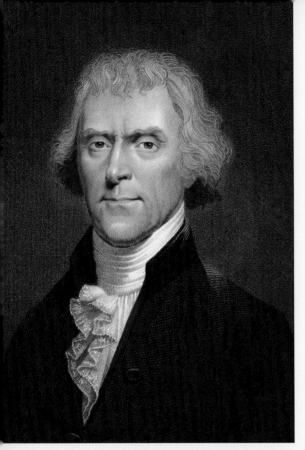

President Thomas Jefferson bought Louisiana from France in 1803.

A Big Purchase

In 1803, French Emperor Napoleon Bonaparte wanted to sell land France owned in North America. The land was called Louisiana. It reached from the Rocky Mountains to the Mississippi River. Jefferson agreed to buy the large piece of land.

Jefferson saw his chance to explore the West. He needed a map of the new **territory**. He wanted to start friendships with the Indians living in the area. Most of all, he wanted to find the Northwest Passage. Jefferson asked his friend Meriwether Lewis to explore Louisiana.

Lewis knew he could not make the trip alone. Lewis wrote a letter to Clark. He asked his friend to be the co-commander. Clark agreed.

Lewis and Clark spent the next year getting ready. Lewis bought supplies. He studied maps and learned how to identify animals and plants. Clark found **interpreters** to help the group talk to the Indians. Together, Lewis and Clark hired more than 30 men for the trip. They called their group the **Corps** of Discovery.

▲ Clark's list of supplies for the trip included flour, biscuits, coffee, and sugar.

Chapter 4

The Journey West Begins

On May 14, 1804, the Corps of Discovery pushed their boats into the Missouri River. The group started about 20 miles (32 kilometers) north of St. Louis, Missouri.

The river was shallow and muddy. The crew could not travel very fast. The men used poles to push their boats along the river. Sometimes, the crew got out and pulled the boats.

The journey was not pleasant. The men worked hard. Swarms of insects bit the men and flew in their mouths. Nobody slept well at night.

The Corps of Discovery pushed down the Missouri River in 1804.

Winter with the Mandans

By October, the group reached what is now North Dakota. The Mandan Indians there were friendly. The explorers built Fort Mandan and spent the winter near the Indian village.

▲ Sacagawea was the only woman on the Lewis and Clark expedition.

During this time, the explorers gained two more interpreters. Touissant Charbonneau was a French fur trader. His wife, Sacagawea, was an American Indian. Lewis and Clark knew Sacagawea would be helpful when the group met Indians.

To the Great Rockies

The group set out again in the spring of 1805. The trip was difficult. Food supplies were low. The Missouri River split, and the group nearly chose the wrong route. Then, the men had to carry everything around the Great Falls.

The explorers' luck changed when they met the Shoshone Indians. Sacagawea knew the Shoshone chief, Cameahwait. He was her brother. He agreed to sell horses to the group.

At the Rocky Mountains, the group expected a single small mountain. Instead, tall peaks rose as far as they could see. There was no river. They finally realized that the Northwest Passage did not exist.

The Shoshone Indians agreed to sell horses to ▼ Lewis and Clark.

The group still needed to reach the Pacific Ocean. They hired Old Toby, a Shoshone, to guide them. Still, they got lost in a snowstorm. It took more than two weeks to pass through the Rockies.

To the Ocean and Back

On the other side of the Rockies, the group followed the Columbia River. This river flowed quickly toward the ocean.

The group met some Chinook Indians. These people wore jewelry made from seashells. The seashells showed that the Pacific Ocean was nearby.

The Corps of Discovery met the Chinook Indians near the Pacific Ocean. ➤

On November 7, 1805, the group passed through a thick fog. When the fog cleared, the explorers could see the Pacific Ocean.

The group built Fort Clatsop in what is now Oregon. The explorers stayed through the winter and left for home in spring.

Lewis and Clark split up for part of the journey home. Lewis went north to the Marias River. Clark went south to the Yellowstone River. They met again west of Fort Mandan.

The trip home took only six months. The Corps of Discovery reached St. Louis in September 1806.

Chapter 5

After the Journey

People were surprised at the group's return in 1806. Many people thought they were dead or lost.

Lewis became governor of the Louisiana Territory in 1807. In October 1809, Lewis was shot while on a trip to Washington, D.C. He may have shot himself. Nobody saw it happen. Lewis died from the bullet wounds.

Clark spent the rest of his life protecting Indians. He became the **superintendent** of Indian Affairs for the United States. He worked to keep peace between American Indians and settlers. Clark died on September 1, 1838.

William Clark became
the superintendent of
Indian Affairs.

Lewis made this drawing of a trout in his journal. ▼

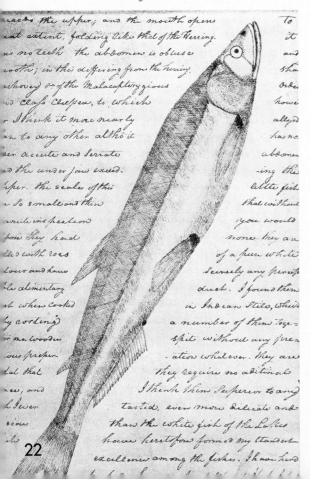

Journals and Maps

Lewis and Clark left behind records of their travels. They kept **journals** of what they saw. They also drew many maps.

The journals described animals and plants that Americans had never seen. These animals included prairie dogs, badgers, elk, and **pronghorn**. Lewis also collected more than 150 different plants.

Lewis and Clark met many American Indians. The explorers recorded the meetings in their journals. They gave beads, medals, and other gifts to the Indian leaders they met.

This 1816 map used information from Lewis and Clark's journey.

The Corps of Discovery's journey changed the United States. The map made by Lewis on the journey helped travelers find their way west. Settlers moved west of the Mississippi River. The Louisiana Territory was divided into many new states. The borders of many of these states were based on rivers and landmarks from Lewis and Clark's maps.

Chapter 6

Lasting Impact

Reminders of Lewis and Clark's journey can be found across the western United States. Lewis and Clark named many plants and landmarks. They called one plant bitterroot. They named the mountains where it grew the Bitterroot Range. Other plants they named include the honeysuckle, the prairie apple, and the salmonberry.

Scientists named some birds in honor of Lewis and Clark. One kind of bird Lewis caught is known as Lewis' woodpecker. Another is named Clark's nutcracker.

These rock formations are part of the Bitterroot Range in Idaho. Lewis and Clark stopped at this spot on August 31, 1805.

25

Remembering Lewis and Clark

On July 1, 2002, President George W. Bush honored Lewis and Clark. He named the years 2003 to 2006 as the Lewis and Clark Bicentennial. Bush wanted to honor the 200th **anniversary** of the Corps of Discovery's trip.

Lewis and Clark's journey to the Pacific Ocean and back is still celebrated. Each year, many people follow the Lewis and Clark National Historic Trail across the West. Along the way, they find sites and landmarks dedicated to the explorers who changed the United States forever.

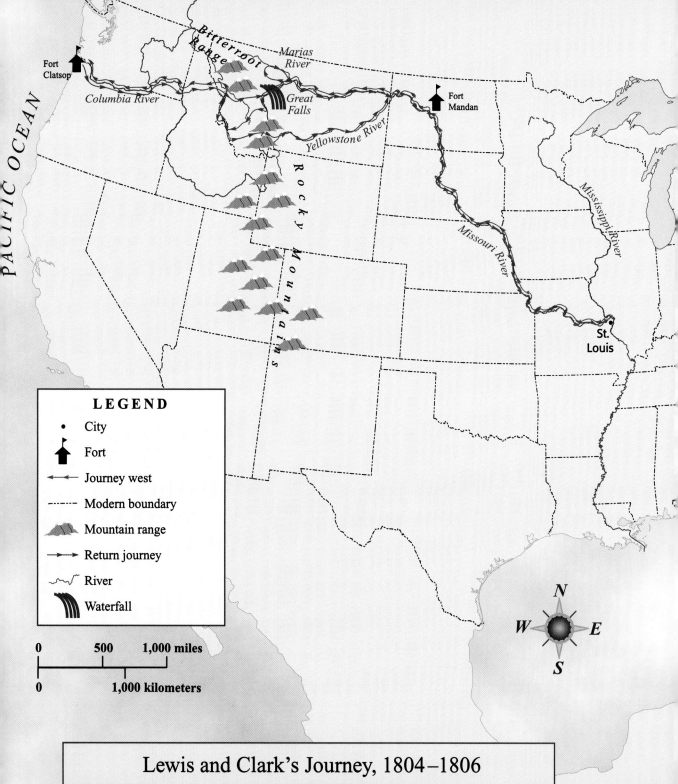

Lewis and Clark's Journey, 1804–1806

LEGEND

- City
- Fort
- Journey west
- Modern boundary
- Mountain range
- Return journey
- River
- Waterfall

0   500   1,000 miles

0   1,000 kilometers

N
W   E
S

PACIFIC OCEAN

Fort Clatsop

Columbia River

Bitterroot Range

Marias River

Great Falls

Yellowstone River

Rocky Mountains

Fort Mandan

Missouri River

Mississippi River

St. Louis

Fast Facts

- President Jefferson bought Louisiana from France in 1803.

- Jefferson asked Meriwether Lewis to explore the newly purchased land.

- Lewis asked William Clark to help him lead the journey.

- Lewis and Clark called their group the Corps of Discovery.

- Lewis and Clark were looking for the Northwest Passage that would connect the Atlantic Ocean to the Pacific Ocean.

- The Corps of Discovery reached the Pacific Ocean in 1805.

- Jefferson made Lewis the governor of the Louisiana Territory in 1807.

- Clark later became the superintendent of Indian Affairs.

Time Line

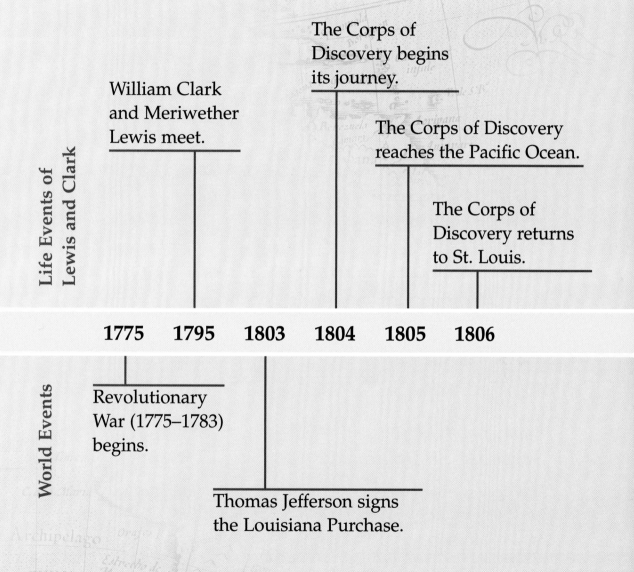

Life Events of Lewis and Clark

William Clark and Meriwether Lewis meet.

The Corps of Discovery begins its journey.

The Corps of Discovery reaches the Pacific Ocean.

The Corps of Discovery returns to St. Louis.

1775 1795 1803 1804 1805 1806

World Events

Revolutionary War (1775–1783) begins.

Thomas Jefferson signs the Louisiana Purchase.

Glossary

anniversary (an-uh-VUR-suh-ree)—a date that people remember because something important happened on that date in the past

corps (KOR)—a group of people acting together or doing the same thing

interpreter (in-TUR-prit-uhr)—a person who can tell others what is said in another language

journal (JUR-nuhl)—a diary in which people regularly write down their thoughts and experiences

pronghorn (PRONG-horn)—an animal of western North America that looks like an antelope and can run very quickly

superintendent (soo-pur-in-TEN-duhnt)—a person who directs or manages an organization

territory (TER-uh-tor-ee)—an area of land that has not yet become a state

Internet Sites

FactHound offers a safe, fun way to find Internet sites related to this book. All of the sites on FactHound have been researched by our staff.

Here's how:
1. Visit *www.facthound.com*
2. Type in this special code **0736826653** for age-appropriate sites. Or enter a search word related to this book for a more general search.
3. Click on the **Fetch It** button.

FactHound will fetch the best sites for you!

Read More

Burger, James P. *Lewis and Clark's Voyage of Discovery.* The Library of the Westward Expansion. New York: PowerKids Press, 2002.

Isaacs, Sally Senzell. *The Lewis and Clark Expedition.* The American Adventure. Chicago: Heinemann Library, 2004.

Quiri, Patricia Ryon. *The Lewis and Clark Expedition.* We the People. Minneapolis: Compass Point Books, 2001.

Ransom, Candice F. *Lewis and Clark.* History Maker Bios. Minneapolis: Lerner, 2003.

Index